WATER

HOW WE CAN PROTECT OUR FRESHWATER

CATHERINE BARR

illustrated by CHRISTIANE ENGEL

CANDLEWICK PRESS

For my friend Sophie, Frank Water ambassador, who introduced
me to the work of this inspiring charity in India and beyond
CB

For Josie Rainbow
CE

Text copyright © 2022 by Catherine Barr
Illustrations copyright © 2022 by Christiane Engel

First US edition 2023
First published by Otter-Barry Books (UK) 2022

Library of Congress Catalog Card Number 2022915350
ISBN 978-1-5362-2886-1

TLF 27 26 25 24 23 22
10 9 8 7 6 5 4 3 2 1

Printed in Dongguan, Guangdong, China

This book was typeset in Mr Dodo and Gill Sans.
The illustrations were done in mixed media.

Candlewick Press
99 Dover Street
Somerville, Massachusetts 02144

www.candlewick.com

Contents

Earth began in a ball of fire. Our burning planet spun around its yellow star, the sun, and in time it cooled. Clouds formed and rain began to fall. Icy space rocks smashed and melted into this changing Earth.

SUN

CLOUDS

RAIN

SEA

RIVERS

This water has made life possible on planet Earth.

This first water collected in dips and hollows and stayed in sunlit pools. It flowed into wide blue rivers and trickled down into dark underground lakes. Most of the rain washed over salty rocks to become the deep blue sea.

The oceans rose and spread out, and this is how Earth became our blue planet.

COMETS

Face the facts

- Earth is the only planet known to have liquid surface water.

- These icy space rocks crashing into early Earth are called comets.

- Today, 70% of Earth's surface is covered in water.

Freshwater is rare

Most water is salty seawater. Just a tiny bit of all the water on our blue planet is freshwater. Today, most of this water is locked in ice.

This ice formed from snow that fell long ago, in periods when the earth was much colder than it is today. In these ice ages, snow packed down to form thick ice that covered huge areas of the planet.

The last ice age created glaciers that still fill high mountain valleys and deep ice sheets that sprawl across Antarctica and the Arctic island of Greenland.

These baby penguins were born on the ice sheet covering Antarctica.

4

Face the facts

- Only 3% of all the water on earth is freshwater.

- About three-quarters of the freshwater on earth exists in glaciers and polar ice sheets.

- The Antarctic ice sheet is the biggest block of ice in the world.

- Today, the world is getting warmer and ice sheets are melting.

The water cycle

All water comes from nature and moves in an endless journey between land and air.

The water cycle begins with the sun, which warms seawater until tiny droplets float up into the air. This water vapor also rises from plants as they breathe. High in the sky, these water droplets cool into clouds that blow over the land. Rising over hills and mountains, the droplets grow until they become so heavy that they fall as rain. The rainwater, melting ice, and rivers flow back into the ocean, beginning the cycle anew.

The water cycle never stops. This means you might drink the same water that dinosaurs gulped 65 million years ago!

SUN

WATER VAPOR

OCEAN

CLOUDS

RAINFALL

Dinosaurs splashed
through ancient wetlands
around the world.

WATER VAPOR

melting
ICE

RIVER

Face the facts

💧 Water has been recycling on earth
for more than four billion years.

💧 A droplet of water can spend nine days in the sky
and then anywhere from a few months to many
hundreds of years moving through the water cycle.

💧 As water moves through the water cycle,
it changes between liquid, gas (water vapor),
and solid ice.

GROUNDWATER

The colors of water

A glass of pure water is colorless, but it is known as *blue water*.
This is the life-giving liquid that tumbles down mountains,
crashes over waterfalls, and runs over and under the land toward
the ocean. Blue water is the liquid water that we can drink and see.

Blue water seeps into soils and is sucked up by plants.
This hidden water is called *green water*. It flows up trees
into branches, leaves, and flowers. All plants need green water
to survive and grow.

Animals, including you, are made of water, too. This precious liquid is in our cells, our skin, and even our bones. Water helps our bodies work and keeps us healthy and strong.

Face the facts

💧 You are about 65% water!

💧 Most plants are 75% water.

💧 Natural freshwater is full of all kinds of invisible microscopic life.

These families are playing in one of New Zealand's many lakes.

Water is life

Freshwater is home to a kaleidoscope of life. From muddy puddles to still ponds, lakes, wetlands, and fast-flowing rivers, plants and animals thrive in very different watery homes. Frogs hop across waterfalls, hippopotamuses sleep in warm pools, fish dart down wide rivers, and snakes weave through flooded forests.

All freshwater dwellers are part of food webs that spread beyond the water's edge. Across wide river basins other creatures also depend on freshwater to survive. Migrating herds of animals and flocks of birds cross dry continents in search of freshwater, and around the world huge wetlands teem with life.

But many of these freshwater habitats are drying up and disappearing. These wild, wet places are some of the most endangered habitats on earth.

These dolphins diving in the Amazon River are an endangered species.

Face the facts

- Every form of life on earth needs water to survive.

- Freshwater habitats are home to more than 15,000 types of fish and more than 4,000 types of frogs!

- Some animals, like salmon and eels, migrate between freshwater and salt water at different times in their lives.

11

The power of water

Water has incredible power. From the steady flow of wide rivers to crashing waterfalls and tumbling streams, water shapes our land. It smooths rocks, carves valleys, and creates landscapes where wildlife and people live.

Throughout history, people have used this natural power to turn waterwheels, drive machines, and make energy. Today, people use water from rivers to flood valleys behind dams. This harnesses the power of huge waterfalls to create electricity.

This renewable energy does not pollute the air, but using water power can damage the natural world. Flooding for dams can block fish migrations and threaten endangered species. In many places, it is destroying habitats and forcing people to abandon their homes and land.

Face the facts

- Rivers power about 17% of the world's electricity.

- More than half of the world's longest rivers are blocked with dams.

- Dams can also be removed, allowing rivers to flow freely again and freshwater life to thrive.

These salmon are leaping up a specially made "fish ladder" in Scotland so they can migrate upriver.

Thirsty food

Farmers need water to bring seeds to life and for animals to drink. They watch the weather and understand the seasons. Since farming began, rain and river water have been irrigating crops.

This family in California is watering crops that otherwise could not grow in this dry landscape.

14

Now most freshwater on earth is used in farming for food.
But farmers everywhere are worried because weather is changing.
Rivers are drying up, droughts are spreading, and farmers are less and less
able to rely on the rain. This is happening because of climate change.

Face the facts

- Climate change today is caused by human activity that adds gases to our atmosphere, trapping heat on Earth.

- These greenhouse gases are released when we burn fossil fuels, destroy forests, graze cows, and grow their feed.

- Climate change makes weather less predictable and more extreme.

- Climate change threatens the survival of animals and people all over the world.

Enough water to share

If we use it carefully, there is enough freshwater on the planet to share. Yet around the world, poorer people have less than they need, mostly because big companies are taking too much.

Gigantic amounts of water are used to grow crops like cotton, sugar, and palm oil. Freshwater is also taken from rivers to cool huge machines in factories and to water golf courses and the gardens of luxury hotels.

These farmers in Mexico are harvesting sugar cane— a water-thirsty crop.

We need water to drink, wash, grow food, create energy, and make clothes and other things we need. But like all other forms of life on earth, we also need healthy rivers and freshwater habitats to survive. Today, freshwater is unequally shared and becoming more polluted, so it is often too dirty to use.

Face the facts

- It takes 60 baths' worth of water to grow the cotton used to make one pair of jeans.

- There are 7.8 billion people on earth, and we all need clean water to survive.

- 844 million people lack access to clean water.

Pollution rising

Big factories and farms take freshwater from nature and pour out used wastewater. In many places, heavy rainfall floods town and city drains. This means that they overflow with dirty water and sewage, which pollutes local rivers.

Toxic substances like oil and chemicals used in agriculture can seep into the earth and pollute groundwater, which many people rely on for drinking water.

These people in India are washing and worshipping by the Ganges, one of the most polluted rivers in the world.

18

Around the world, polluted water is spilling into freshwater habitats where animals and people live. It is poisoning the water people drink and killing freshwater wildlife.

Face the facts

- Around half of the wastewater around the world is untreated, which means it may be harmful to wildlife and people.

- Every year, millions of people get sick from unsafe water.

- Scientists are investigating the threat to wildlife from rising levels of plastics in freshwater habitats.

19

Girl power

Many families in poorer countries do not have enough water. Every day, women and girls walk for hours to find and carry water back to their villages in heavy pots and buckets.

Often this water is polluted, so whole villages share dirty water that poses a real risk of disease. Droughts created by climate change cause even more water stress. Spending so much time collecting water means that girls miss school, and millions grow up without a good education.

But simple wells and taps can bring clean water to rural villages, giving girls a proper chance to go to school and mothers the time to work. This makes families healthier and communities stronger. Access to water can change and save lives.

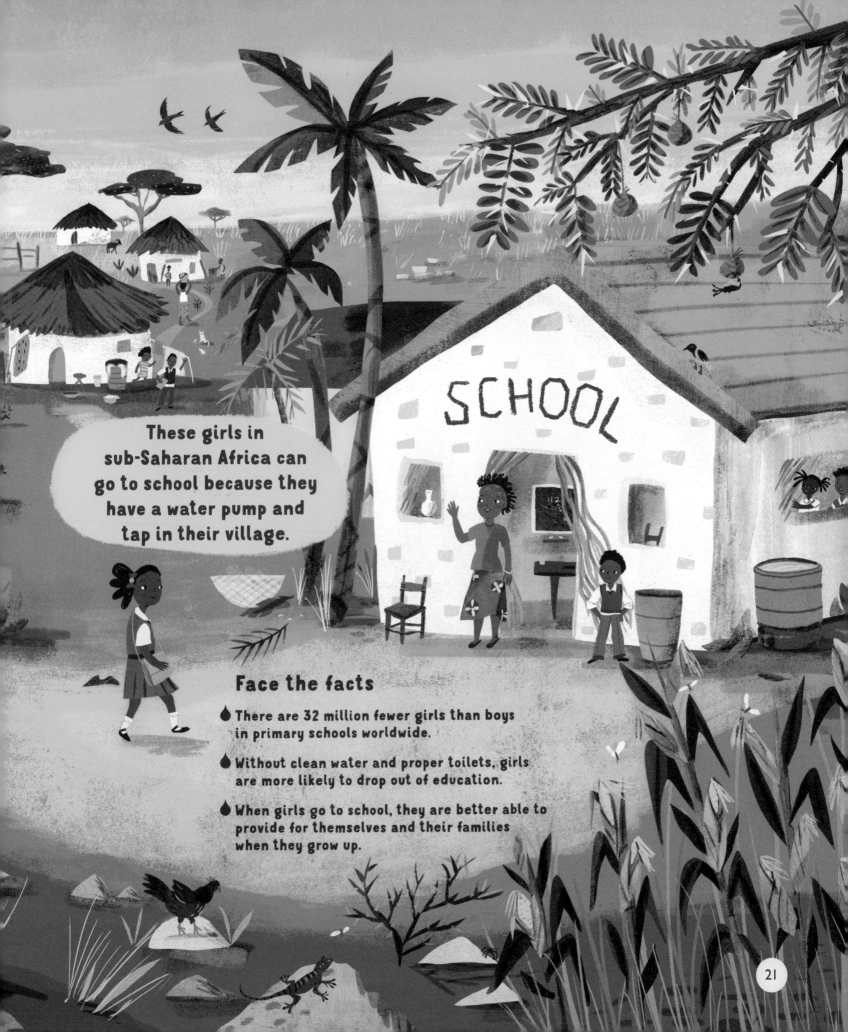

These girls in sub-Saharan Africa can go to school because they have a water pump and tap in their village.

Face the facts

- There are 32 million fewer girls than boys in primary schools worldwide.

- Without clean water and proper toilets, girls are more likely to drop out of education.

- When girls go to school, they are better able to provide for themselves and their families when they grow up.

Our precious water

Water is life. Freshwater springs, bubbles, and flows with some of the most wonderful life on earth. It makes up most of our bodies, and, like all other forms of life, we completely rely on it to stay alive.

But today there is a freshwater crisis on planet Earth. As the human population grows, as our climate changes and rivers are polluted, it is more and more difficult for people and animals to find the clean freshwater they need to survive.

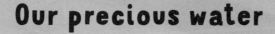

These protesters in Cape Town, South Africa, are asking farmers, businesses, and families to save water to stop the city from running dry.

WATER IS LIFE

Change is Now

Save our WATER

CLIMATE EMERGENCY ACT NOW!

DAY Zero is coming!

Together, we can protect and share the precious freshwater on our blue planet. It's time to act—to make sure there is always enough clean water for all life on planet Earth.

Face the facts

- Agricultural waste is the leading source of water pollution.
- One-third of all freshwater species are threatened by extinction.
- More than three-quarters of all freshwater animals have disappeared since 1970.
- Only a tiny part of all the water we use is recycled.

A bath uses about 30 gallons of water, but a shower uses only about 17 gallons on average.

Using a fully loaded dishwasher saves more water than washing everything by hand.

Americans flush the toilet 664 billion times per year, using 1.4 trillion gallons of water.

Use environmentally friendly cleaning products.

Use a rain barrel to catch rainwater to water your plants, clean the car, and wash windows.

Don't wait for the tap to run cold— save up to 2½ gallons of water a day!

- Eat less meat and dairy. A plain hamburger can take 680 gallons of water to produce—that's about 22 baths!

- Contact a local wildlife organization to find out how you can help protect freshwater habitats.

How can I use water wisely?
Take action to shrink your *water footprint!*

- Almost everything takes water to make, so if we buy less, we shrink our water footprint.

- Visit your local river or lake to discover the animals and plants that live there. Is it home to any endangered species?

- To reduce waste, use less plastic, recycle, and reuse the things you buy.

- Get involved—join a climate action group!

25

It's Water Action Decade!

The United Nations (UN) has declared 2018–2028 the Water Action Decade. That's 10 years of special focus to achieve safe and affordable drinking water for all by 2030.

LEARN Read this book to discover the story of freshwater around the world.

SHARE Share this book with your friends, family, and school to start conversations about water.

ACT Use the ideas in this book to save water and help protect freshwater habitats locally and globally.

◆ **WORLD WATER DAY: MARCH 22**
   worldwaterday.org

◆ **WORLD TOILET DAY: NOVEMBER 19**
   worldtoiletday.info

Find out how you can help people save water in other countries, too!
   wateraid.org
   water.org

Governments, agriculture businesses, and industry must take the lead in protecting freshwater. But by sharing this book and telling stories about freshwater, you, too, can make change happen. Together, we must protect freshwater to save life on earth.